D1710298

Discovering JOBS

Jobs If You Like
MUSIC

James Roland

ReferencePoint
Press®

San Diego, CA

© 2022 ReferencePoint Press, Inc.
Printed in the United States

For more information, contact:
ReferencePoint Press, Inc.
PO Box 27779
San Diego, CA 92198
www.ReferencePointPress.com

LIBRARY OF CONGRESS CATALOGING-IN-PUBLICATION DATA

Names: Roland, James, author.
Title: Jobs if you like music / James Roland.
Description: San Diego : ReferencePoint Press, 2021. | Series: Discovering
   jobs | Includes bibliographical references and index.
Identifiers: LCCN 2021035603 (print) | LCCN 2021035604 (ebook) | ISBN
   9781678202262 (library binding) | ISBN 9781678202279 (ebook)
Subjects: LCSH: Music--Vocational guidance--Juvenile literature.
Classification: LCC ML3795 .R667 2021 (print) | LCC ML3795 (ebook) | DDC
   780.23--dc23
LC record available at https://lccn.loc.gov/2021035603
LC ebook record available at https://lccn.loc.gov/2021035604

CONTENTS

INTRODUCTION: A LIFE IN SONG

Lady Gaga became a star overnight with the release of her first album, *The Fame*. But that instant stardom actually started eighteen years earlier, when she was four years old, taking piano lessons and practicing on an upright piano that used to belong to her grandparents.

After studying voice and playing in bands throughout her teen years, at age twenty-one in 2007, Lady Gaga signed with a record label, and the following year, *The Fame* was released. The album of original music kicked off a career making pop hits, packing arenas during world tours, becoming a respected activist for environmental issues and LGBTQ rights, and acting in film and television. When she won the Academy Award for Best Original Song, "Shallow" in 2019, she said in her acceptance speech, "This is hard work. I've worked hard for a long time, and it's not about winning—but what it's about is not giving up. If you have a dream, fight for it."[1]

The Music World Upended

While any career requires a certain amount of hard work, perseverance, and talent, that is especially true of musical artists and others in the music industry. The competition, changing audience tastes, and the difficulty of just getting that first big break, let alone maintaining a successful career, can be daunting. But even more overwhelming was the COVID-19 pandemic, which upended the music world in unprecedented ways.

Broadway theaters went dark for more than a year. Worldwide concert tours by Harry Styles, the Foo Fighters, Taylor Swift, and other superstars were scrapped. Orchestras and operas shut down or offered online performances. Recording studios fell silent. Curtains never opened on countless high school plays and concerts. The world grew quieter and sadder. "It's chilling we lost an entire year, and that's every single touring act internationally," says Adriane Biondo, a longtime Miami-based touring manager for Mariah Carey and other performers. "The venues, the folks that work at the venues. That's everything from trucks to buses to the hotels all the way to the mom and pop pizza joints and restaurants that are around the venues. Everything changed."[2]

Creative and Resourceful

And though some normalcy returned to parts of the world in 2021, the lessons of the pandemic will linger. Performers and others in the music industry learned how to be more resourceful in making and releasing music. Music educators taught their students and conducted performances remotely. Songwriters took advantage of the lockdown to spend more time at the piano, while producers and DJs concentrated on the creative sides of their jobs, too. Leonard Jacobs, interim executive director of the Jamaica Center for Arts & Learning in New York City, converted the center's annual dance festival from a live, in-person event to a filmed show distributed online. He also oversaw the construction of a semipermanent stage outside the center that is used for rehearsals and performances that people in the community can enjoy as they pass by or gather for a little outdoor entertainment. The new "hybrid" model for all of the center's activities, Jacobs says, is likely here to stay. "Artists are never going to be kept down," he told the *Queens Chronicle* newspaper in 2021. "Artists are never going to be kept from doing their work. It forced everybody to be inventive, resourceful, brave, smart and strategic."[3]

Even without a global health crisis or other extraordinary challenge, people in the music business have always found creative ways to do their work. In the years before the internet, performers used to have to hope for their big chance or work for years to get an opportunity to break through, but now they can turn to

YouTube, TikTok, SoundCloud, and other online platforms and reach millions of people overnight. Stars like the Weeknd, Justin Bieber, Lil Nas X, and Shawn Mendes all got their start releasing their music via homemade videos online. "This is the democratization of the music industry that people were hoping for when social media first became available,"[4] Bill Werde, director of Syracuse University's music industry program and a former editor with *Billboard*, told *Time* magazine in 2019.

As much as the music industry changes, talent and dedication are still at the heart of every music-related job around the world. People who love music may not end up touring the world and winning awards like Lady Gaga or Lil Nas X, but they may find a way to have a rewarding career with music at its center.

PERFORMER

In the musical professions, performers make their living as singers, musicians, or dancers. When people talk about performers in the music industry, they probably think of superstars like Beyoncé or Billie Eilish. But for every world-famous artist selling out giant concert halls and arenas and cranking out hit songs year after year, there are many more singers, dancers, and musicians who are not famous but still make a decent living doing something they love.

A Few Facts

Typical Earnings
About $31 an hour, but much less or much more for some

Educational Requirements
No formal education required, though many performers have years of training

Personal Qualities
Talent, creativity, motivation, resilience, confidence, discipline, and collaborative skills

Work Settings
Rehearsal and recording studios, clubs, concert halls

What Does a Performer Do?

A performer's job is to entertain an audience. Performers include rock drummers, violinists in symphony orchestras, and trumpet players in New Orleans jazz clubs. They dance in Broadway musicals, eight shows a week for months at a time. They are opera singers, rappers, and folk singers. Some go on worldwide tours, and others perform only in their hometowns. They perform at weddings, play the organ during baseball games, and delight holiday crowds by dancing in *The Nutcracker*.

Singers, musicians, and dancers reach their audiences through recorded or live performances. They spend much more of their time learning and rehearsing material than they do actually performing it before an audience or recording it in a studio. Singers perform with bands or orchestras, as solo acts, or if they like playing characters while they sing, in operas or musical theater. Likewise, dancers perform in musicals, in ballets, and with professional dance troupes. Musicians can be session musicians who are hired to play with a recording artist, or they can perform in orchestras, with bands, or as solo acts.

The Workday

Whether they dance, play musical instruments, sing, or do a mix of these, performers have one thing in common: they spend hours every day, or most days, practicing their craft. The workday for most performers usually begins with some kind of warm-up: vocal exercises for singers, stretching for dancers, and some scales and other exercises for musicians. Dancers with the Atlanta Ballet, for example, start with a ninety-minute class that includes a warm-up and then work on refining techniques. That is followed by four to six hours of rehearsals, and then on some nights, a performance to end the day.

Colorado Ballet dancer Sharon Wehner puts in a similarly grueling rehearsal schedule. "As a professional ballet dancer, I often get questions from non-dancers about what a work day/week/

month looks like," she wrote in the dance blog *4dancers*. "This is usually followed by a look of surprise when I say that I dance six to nine hours a day, five to six days per week, an average of 45 weeks a year."[5]

A professional musician who works for an orchestra may have a less demanding formal rehearsal schedule than some other performers, but individual practice hours add up. Douglas Yeo, a trombone player with the Boston Symphony Orchestra, wrote on his website that the four two-and-a-half-hour rehearsals and four performances each week were a demanding but appealing schedule. "If a player chooses not to teach or engage in work outside the orchestra, it is possible to be home for three meals a day on most days of the week and enjoy a 'work week' of about 20 hours on the job. Of course, individual practice adds up to make a full work week, but such practice can be done on a flexible schedule and usually at home,"[6] he wrote.

Education and Training

Many professional musicians started out in music when they were young. They took dance lessons as children, played an instrument in the school band, or sang in the school chorus or a church choir. Or they picked up a guitar and taught themselves some chords as a teenager. Many had private lessons as well.

While some musicians are self-taught, a music education at the college level can be helpful in launching a professional career. Darrah Carr, board of study coordinator for the dance program at the State University of New York at Purchase, says:

> In a college program, it's pretty much a given that you'll be dancing a lot and will graduate in great physical shape, but your curriculum is set up to progressively provide so many other benefits. Things like education on injury prevention and developing a warm-up routine will actually enable you to have a longer career. It's very difficult to replicate such comprehensive training on your own.[7]

Skills and Personality

It is a given that a musical performer must have a lot of talent and creativity to succeed. But there are plenty of other qualities a musical entertainer must possess. Survival in this business requires a thick skin and confidence to spare in the face of fickle audiences, harsh critics, and countless auditions that end in rejection. The legendary Aretha Franklin, known as the Queen of Soul, once said, "Be your own artist, and always be confident in what you're doing. If you're not going to be confident, you might as well not be doing it."[8]

Other important attributes include dedication, patience, and a willingness to objectively view your work, see what needs improving, and then put in the time to practice or learn new skills and material. No matter how accomplished a musician becomes, the need for practice never goes away. "If I have a lot of repertoire to learn, I'll practice for up to eight hours in a day,"[9] world-renowned violinist Sarah Chang told an interviewer.

Working Conditions

Working conditions for musical performers run the gamut from seedy clubs to world-class performing arts halls. They work and rehearse in home recording studios, basements, and garages. They also work in private recording studios, rehearsal halls, and just about anywhere else they can find to play with other musicians or reach an audience. Dancers spend much of their time training and rehearsing in dance studios. If they are cast members in a show, they also spend much of their time in the theater.

Concerts and other musical performances are usually held at night, so a typical workday for a working musician often starts in the late morning or early afternoon and finishes late at night. Being a musical performer often means a lot of travel. Some artists choose to live and work in the same area, while others tour with a band or a show. Life on the road away from home and in a different city every night can be difficult, but many artists say it is the only way to master the art of performing in front of an audience.

Whether playing at a music festival (pictured), club, concert, or even a party or wedding, the job of a performer is to entertain an audience. Musical performers sing, dance, or play instruments—and some do all three.

"There's no shortcuts in rock & roll," says Taylor Momsen, singer with the band the Pretty Reckless. "You have to tour for ten years, to go out there night after night and play. We weren't looking for shortcuts. We wanted to put the work in to do it right, to try to be great, to attempt to get as close to that as possible."[10]

Employers and Earnings

When a musical artist is looking for work, the day often begins with a nervous but hopeful search through job listings or, for some, a check-in with their agent. Landing a job in music is more than just having the right résumé and doing well in an interview. Entertainers have to nail their auditions. If all goes well, they sign a contract with a symphony orchestra, ballet company, opera company, theatrical production, or other arts organization. If not, the quest for more audition opportunities continues.

Telling Stories in Song

"As a singer, I truly believe that my job is to communicate and tell the stories that sometimes are difficult for people to tell for themselves."

—Grammy, Emmy, and Tony winner Cynthia Erivo

Quoted in Mesfin Fekadu, "With Much Respect, Cynthia Erivo Takes on Queen of Soul," AP, March 1, 2021. https://apnews.com.

Performers who are not part of a larger music company are self-employed, playing gigs when they can or looking to be under contract for some financial security. That is not always easy to obtain. Many self-employed performers need to work a second job in order to make enough money to live on. Those side jobs are what allow performers to stick with their passion for music. For Travis McClung, a stage actor and singer in New York City, waiting tables on the side was a necessity. "It was a sense of security," he told the Associated Press in 2020. "It let me stay in New York City, pay the rent here."[11]

On the other hand, musicians in a major symphony orchestra, for example, are full-time employees with contracts that may run a year at a time or may last for several years. Major orchestras pay musicians more than $100,000 a year, with principals (the leader of each orchestra section) earning much more. Researching the likely income stream for a particular musical performer career track can be helpful, so artists know from the beginning what to realistically expect.

Future Outlook

Job growth for musical performers lags behind many other professions, yet there is never a shortage of people hoping to turn their passion into a profession. The rise of online platforms has allowed many performers to do just that. They can build and sustain an audience on their own without having to wait to be discovered by a record label executive.

People crave entertainment. If there is one takeaway from the COVID-19 pandemic and how it devastated the music industry, it is that when the chance to see live performances became possible again, fans flocked to concert halls, theaters, arenas, and clubs. In an interview with ABC News in February 2021, Virginia musician James Potter said he believed fan response was about something deeper than enjoying a night of live music. "You become incredibly grateful for basic human needs and for the soul food that sustains you," he said. "And that's precisely where the arts come in. They minister to the heart and the mind in crisis."[12]

Find Out More

How to Break into Musical Theater, *Backstage*
www.backstage.com/magazine/article/become-musical-theater-actor-4572
Find out more about the many types of musical theater (it is not all on Broadway), as well as the education and training that will help prepare actors for their first professional auditions and onstage careers. There are also plenty of tips about how to put together a résumé and a reel to show off a performer's singing, dancing, and acting skills.

Kennedy Center Education
www.kennedy-center.org/education
Learn about programs and educational opportunities for students of all ages interested in music and the performing arts. Find articles about becoming a professional singer or musician. The Kennedy Center, a Washington, DC, landmark and leader in performing arts education, also provides internships for students and information about music internships elsewhere.

Tips on Starting a Career as a Musician, Making Music
https://makingmusicmag.com/starting-a-career-musician
This article provides some helpful ideas and suggestions for wannabe musicians, as well as links to other interesting articles about various instruments, music theory, and starting a band.

COMPOSER/SONGWRITER

Composers and songwriters are creative people who write music to be performed by others. They have similar talents, but the nature of their work is often very different. A composer's job is to provide the music for a filmed, recorded, or theatrical production. He or she works in support of another's artistic vision. Songwriters typically write the music or lyrics or both for songs that will be performed by singers and musicians.

A Few Facts

Typical Earnings
Average annual salary of $52,000

Educational Requirements
No formal education required, although many have a music degree

Personal Qualities
Creativity, determination, willingness to always be learning

Work Settings
At home or in a recording studio

What Does a Composer/ Songwriter Do?

When a movie theater gradually darkens, and the screen comes alive with light and action, this is usually the cue for the music to begin. The musical accompaniment to any piece of entertainment that needs a soundtrack is called a score. And that score was composed by someone who had seen a "rough cut" of the film and talked with the director and producers about the kind of music needed for each scene. In some cases, composers begin writing a score based on only having read the script.

Composers also write all kinds of other music. They write the bits of music that play under the introduction to a podcast, during a car commercial, or while the heroes and heroines in a video game are beginning their quest.

And some composers with a theatrical background write scores and songs for musicals and operas—composing both music and lyrics. For many composers, working in their fields is a natural extension of a lifelong love affair with films or stage musicals. Tony Award–winning composer Maury Yeston says his work as a Broadway veteran is not that different from his approach as a teenager learning his craft. "At 10 or 11, I saw 'My Fair Lady' and I knew I wanted to do that," he says. "I began sitting and writing music at the age of 16 in high school, then in Footlights [student musical-comedy troupe] at Yale and Cambridge. My lifestyle has never changed. I'm a perpetual student and perpetual teacher and writer of music."[13]

Songwriters typically pen songs for singers, rappers, or bands to perform live or record on an album. In addition to writing the melody and lyrics, songwriters often record demos so artists who may be interested in acquiring the song can get an idea how the song will sound. Songwriters usually stick to a genre, such as country music or rhythm and blues, and write songs hoping to get singers and producers to listen to the tunes and include the songs on their next project.

Sometimes a songwriter will be hired to work with a performer. That is how Julia Michaels, who started selling songs to the producers of TV shows such as *The Hills* and Disney Channel's *Austin & Ally* as a teenager, wound up collaborating with Selena Gomez on her album *Revival*. "I get so much more joy out of other people singing what I've written than I do singing them myself," Michaels says. "I don't mind being anonymous. I don't want the responsibility of being an artist and people knowing everything about my life. Being a writer, there is some pressure, but it's not even close to what some of the artists deal with."[14]

The Workday

Film composer Wes Hughes spends almost as much time repeatedly watching the movie he is scoring and talking with the director as he does at his keyboard writing the actual score. In an interview for California video production company Wistia's career education program, Hughes said he watches a film five to twenty times, taking detailed notes about camera angles, costumes, and scenery; graphing the narrative arc; and trying to better understand the themes and style of the work. Then he goes on a hike or runs errands as the ideas crash around in his mind. "By the end of this process," he says, "music usually pops into my head on its own. I rarely write any music down before I absorb the film because otherwise the music ends up making it more like a music video, which serves no one. Often, a film will have something special about it that the director wants to draw attention to and this will inspire my approach."[15]

Songwriters have a less complicated job, but it is professionally just as challenging. They usually write at home with a guitar, piano, or synthesizer, as well as a pad of paper and pen or pencil, hoping inspiration leads them to a great song. Songwriters also listen to a lot of music, listening for the sounds and styles that need to be incorporated in their next effort. When they are happy with a new song, they will record a demo of it or have someone else record it. That demo can be the ticket to selling a song or at least having someone offer to hear more of their work.

Education and Training

Songwriters usually start out playing an instrument, such as a piano or guitar. That foundation in music can be enough to allow creative people to try a hand at songwriting. For people who write poetry, taking that next step and turning those words into lyrics with a melody does not seem too daunting.

Many songwriters find a mentor or a collaborator with songwriting experience to learn from. But some songwriters take a slightly more formal approach. Songwriting courses are taught online and in colleges. And for film composers, a formal education in composing is almost a requirement in order to learn all there is about scoring and about the entertainment business. The University of Southern California (USC) Thornton School of Music is

Everything Is an Audition

"One of the keys to finding work is to remember that composers, no matter how established, are always auditioning. Every piece of work is a calling card and an audition piece for the next one. Every performance you give is a representation of your artistry."

—Composer Jeremy Borum

Jeremy Borum, "Finding Work as a Composer," ASCAP. www.ascap.com.

considered one of the best programs for composers in the nation, says longtime Motown composer and producer Lamont Dozier, an instructor at USC for many years. "It has so many applicants and the people that come there are really talented," he says. "We turn away hundreds of people every year because they're very strict about who they [accept], and their teaching is very rigid, [so] the people who want to be there have to be there talent-wise and have to have love and dedication."[16]

Skills and Personality

Songwriters and composers need to be musically creative and talented. They also need to be able to judge their own work critically and take criticism from others without becoming defeated or discouraged. This means being tough skinned, while at the same time listening to criticisms or judgments that may make them better writers.

Given the competition in the music industry, healthy doses of determination and patience are also vital. "The career span for composers is so slow-moving and long-term," says opera composer Philip Venables. "You've got to stick at it."[17]

Working Conditions

While much of the composing is done at home, composers also spend a considerable amount of time meeting with filmmakers at

Creating Something New

"If somebody said to me, 'You can only do one thing in show business for the rest of your whole life. What will it be?' I would say, 'I'll write songs.' To me, it's like putting something in the world today that wasn't there yesterday that will still be there tomorrow. That's my favorite thing I do."

—Songwriter and singer Dolly Parton

Lydia Hutchinson, "Dolly Parton," *Performing Songwriter*, November 3, 2010. https://performingsongwriter.com.

their offices or at the studio. And when it is time to actually put that score on the soundtrack with a full orchestra (or whatever group of musicians that is involved), a composer will work closely with the sound crew, editor, and director during lengthy recording sessions at the studio.

During the COVID-19 pandemic, filmmakers and composers had to get creative to finish their products. In recording the soundtrack for the 2020 film *Mank*, composer Atticus Ross conducted individual sessions with dozens of musicians who played and recorded their parts solo at home. "When it got time to record the orchestra and the big band, it was literally each musician in their kitchen or living room or whatever, and then assembling those parts together into what you hear in the film," he said in an interview in the *Hollywood Reporter*. "All in all, I'm incredibly proud of how it turned out."[18]

Unless songwriters have been hired to pen songs for someone, they do not have the deadlines that composers do. Songwriters work at their own pace, either at a home studio or with a singer or musician in a recording studio.

Employers and Earnings

Music composers make an average of $52,000 a year, according to the Bureau of Labor Statistics. The employment website

ZipRecruiter reports about the same annual income for song-writers, with the typical range running from about $17,500 to $122,000. Neither profession provides steady, long-term employment with a single employer.

Instead, composers are hired by filmmakers, television producers, video game manufacturers, theatrical producers, and anyone else who needs music for their productions. Composers sign a contract to deliver a score by a certain date. The score belongs to the studio or production company, but a composer can earn royalties, which are payments composers receive whenever their work is performed.

Songwriters, who are usually self-employed, typically do not sell their songs; rather, they license them to a singer, record label, or other entity. After that, there are three income streams that make it possible to earn more money from the same song. The first is a mechanical royalty, which is the sale of a song on an album or digital download. Each sale or download means 9.1 cents for the songwriter, though that is often split with the music publishing company and any cowriters. For example, if a songwriter's mechanical royalty works out to 5 cents per download, a song that is downloaded 100,000 times brings in $5,000. A million downloads earns the songwriter $50,000.

The second is a performance royalty, meaning the songwriter receives a small fee every time a song is played in concert or on a radio broadcast or online streaming service. The third is a sync fee, which is paid when a song is licensed for use in a movie, TV show, YouTube video, or other similar purpose.

Future Outlook

While songwriting and composing have and always will be competitive fields to work in, the massive amount of entertainment content produced every year equates to an ongoing need for songs and scores. In 2020, for example, there were nearly three hundred streaming services, presenting original movies, series, news, and much more—all of which incorporated music into their programming. And there is no reason to think that demand for new content is going to subside. For talented people willing to work hard and collaborate with singers, musicians, filmmakers, video game producers, theatrical companies, and anyone else producing new artistic work, there will be audiences waiting and listening for the stories songwriters and composers are ready to tell.

Find Out More

Majoring in Music
https://majoringinmusic.com
Learn about collegiate music programs, scholarships, summer programs for teens, and information about a variety of careers in the music industry. The site also contains helpful articles on auditioning, rehearsing, and many other topics of interest to student musicians, songwriters, singers, and composers.

Musical America Worldwide
www.musicalamerica.com
Get information about careers in the music industry, music schools, and contests for songwriting, composing, and performing. The site also includes a wide network of artists, managers, and other industry professionals offering their services.

Nashville Songwriters Association International
www.nashvillesongwriters.com
The site includes information about songwriting contests, how writers get paid, tips for songwriters, and more. The focus is on writing for country music and the Nashville music scene, but there is information that can help songwriters in any genre.

MUSIC PRODUCER

Music producers oversee the recording of an artist's music. A producer might work on one song or a whole album. While the specific duties of a producer vary from person to person and project to project, in general producers tend to have their hands in both the creative and business sides of the recording industry. A producer creates an environment that allows artists to express themselves, while also making sure the recording sessions are on time and within the budget set by whoever is financing the project. In many cases the record label is paying the bills, but some artists finance their own recordings.

A producer wears many hats and has to make countless decisions, but for creative people who enjoy working with a variety of artists and helping them make the best music possible, it can be a very rewarding job. "I love being a producer for bands," rock producer Sam Carlson told an interviewer. "It's kind of like playing with someone else's dog because you're there for the best part, like where the band is at their most creative and having a good time and they're getting into the process."[19]

A Few Facts

Typical Earnings
Average annual salary of $53,000

Educational Requirements
No formal education required, but a bachelor's degree in music or music production could be helpful

Personal Qualities
Good communicator, decisive, creative

Work Settings
Recording studio

What Does a Music Producer Do?

From a big commercial recording studio in Los Angeles to a tiny studio in West Texas to a singer's home studio in Nashville, music producers create songs and records in collaboration with musicians, recording engineers, and other individuals—all with the goal of making good music even better. The producer oversees the entire process, including the selection of engineers, musicians or backup singers that may be needed, arranging the lyrics or melodies, making demos, editing performances, and making sure everything is done within the budget.

Producers are creators, collaborators, and experimenters who must be willing to try new ideas, toss out the ones that do not work, and experiment in the studio. Producers also tend to be perfectionists. "If you hit play and the playback is not changing your life, then to me, it's not a job well done,"[20] says the Grammy Award–winning producer Illangelo in an article about producing the Weeknd's *After Hours*.

The primary responsibilities of a music producer usually start with helping an artist select the songs that will be on an album and then working on song and production arrangements. Decisions have to be made about when to bring the chorus in, whether to change a verse or add string instruments, whether percussion should be louder, and many other aspects of recording a song.

Producers also work with artists on selecting the right studio for recording and hiring other singers or musicians, as well as putting together the team of recording engineers, sound mixers, and other technicians. Sometimes the producer doubles as the recording engineer or as an extra musician. In a hip-hop recording session, the producer could be making the beats and building tracks. Some producers are involved in every detail of the song selection and recording process, while others work with artists who want to make all the decisions, leaving the producer to focus more on the less-creative parts of the job, such as budgeting and scheduling.

And with up-and-coming musical acts, the producer can play the role of coach or teacher. That is how it is with Texas-based heavy metal record producer Joshua Lopez, who does everything from replacing bass guitar strings to advising a guitarist on a better hand position for strumming. "Every single band that's gone through [Widowmaker Studios], I'm coaching them through it," he told KVEO News in Brownsville, Texas. "What I do is tell them what they're doing wrong and show them how to do it right."[21]

The Workday

A producer's day can start early in the morning and last well into the night or into the next day. Many artists and producers like to work straight through without taking a long break if they feel their creative juices flowing. When an artist is recording songs for an album, the producer sometimes puts in longer days than the artist, working after the artist has recorded various tracks and left the studio. The producer and recording engineers experiment with the recordings, speeding up or slowing down various parts, making some sections louder and others quieter. "It's not a nine-to-five job," says producer Matt Ross-Spang. "Sometimes you work through the night. Sometimes you work months without a day off. It's because you love what you do. If this isn't 100 percent your passion, it's probably not the right thing for you."[22]

Supporting the Artists

"Essentially, all I do is help an artist record a song. What that is changes a lot. Usually it involves sitting in rehearsals, discussing the songs, suggesting changes and creating a plan for how we will record the song. In the studio, you may decide which drum kit you use, how to tune it for each song and how many microphones to put on it. You may change instruments and amplifiers for each song, and even for different parts within the one song. You can also record the vocals in many different ways. The producer makes all of these decisions. Sometimes, my job is just a matter of setting up the mics and pressing record. I guess it's knowing how to approach each project."

—Australian producer Magoo

Quoted in Bec Wolfers, "A Week in the Life of . . . a Music Producer, Magoo," Music Industry Inside Out. https://musicindustryinsideout.com.

But some producers work differently, spending less time in the studio because long days can make everyone involved tired and unproductive. Canadian producer JP Remillard says he might spend only a few hours on the production of a track, using the rest of his time tweaking or "micro-editing" the song. "I love to have the people I coach over at the studio, and sometimes friends will visit, too," he wrote on his company's website. "The time I spend with others in studio is extremely valuable, because I'm nourished by the ideas we exchange and the music they share."[23]

A producer also spends days out of the studio, meeting with record label executives to work out a recording budget and time-table for the production. As the recording and production go along, the producer may meet with representatives from the label and play them tracks being considered for an album. In between projects, a producer may spend days listening to demos from artists interested in hiring that producer. Writing and arranging songs prior to recording can also take up a lot of hours.

Education and Training

A music producer needs to learn all aspects of the recording industry, from the software used by recording engineers and the various aspects of recording and mixing sound to market research that reveals what audiences want. And of course, producers need to know music. Learning to play multiple instruments is helpful so that a producer can more easily arrange the parts to be played by other musicians.

A formal education in music or music production is helpful. Many producers are also songwriters. Taking business and accounting courses is also useful in developing and sticking to a budget.

Learning the trade as a sound engineer is a great place to start, just to become familiar with the technology. Shadowing professional engineers or getting an internship can provide a good look at what is involved in recording and producing. Recording local artists with whatever audio gear is available is also useful hands-on experience. Many producers are or were performers in their own right. Artists who pay close attention to the recording process can learn skills that they can then apply as producers for others.

Skills and Personality

Organization, patience, and creativity are three of the most important traits for a music producer. A producer has to be able to manage many people with different personalities and skills, while keeping a production on time and within the budget. It can also be a challenge working with artists who are headstrong or second-guess themselves or are struggling to deliver a great performance. Finding creative solutions to problems is also a necessity for a producer, who must often come up with ideas on the fly.

The two main skills a music producer needs are the abilities to arrange a song and to oversee the recording so that the final product is as good as or better than how it sounded in the mind of the musician. But it is not just about the technology. People skills are critical, since producers deal with artists singing and playing their hearts out as well as engineers, record company representatives, and everyone else with their own interest in the finished product. "You really need to be a people person," says Ross-Spang. "You really need to be a good listener. And you really need to gain people's trust and make them feel at ease."[24]

Working Conditions

Much of a producer's time is spent working in a recording studio with singers, musicians, engineers, and other technicians, as well as record label representatives and other interested parties. Many studios are windowless places designed for optimal acoustics and greater focus on what is happening inside rather than outside. But a producer who is passionate about making music does not mind one bit. Dr. Dre, the famous rapper-turned-producer who has worked with 50 Cent, Eminem, Kendrick Lamar, and many others, once said, "I've gone 79 hours without sleep, creating. When that flow is going, it's almost like a high. You don't want it to stop. You don't want to go to sleep for fear of missing something."[25]

Employers and Earnings

Producers are usually hired by a record label or an artist, whoever is financing the recording. Up-and-coming artists without a record deal usually do not have a lot of money to spend on a producer. But working for little or no money is pretty typical for producers starting out. They have to build a body of work so they can be hired by record labels and artists who have the money to spend. One producer might earn $25,000 a year, and another producer working with big-name acts might make millions of dollars. The average annual salary for a music producer is about $53,000, according to the employment website Glassdoor. "If you're in this job seeking big money, you're in the wrong field," jazz producer Zev Feldman said in an interview on the Careers in Music website. "Things naturally progress over time, and you'll get promotions along the way and build a career."[26] But a love for music, producing and the creative process should be the priority, rather than dreams of a fast track to fame and riches.

Future Outlook

As digital technology makes it easier to make and distribute new music, more music is being produced and released than ever before. That means more artists will need talented producers to help them achieve their creative visions. And while there was a time not that long ago when becoming a producer meant learning on the job in a studio that happened to offer a young person a break, now recording software can be purchased by anyone. Many of the tools of the trade are right there on a laptop computer ready to be put to work making good music great.

Find Out More

Careers in Music

www.careersinmusic.com

Visitors to this website can learn from longtime professional producers about what it takes to get into the business and stay there. Visitors can also read about the skills music producers need and the challenges of working long hours in a fascinating and creative profession.

Majoring in Music

https://majoringinmusic.com

Learn what to look for in a college music production program and what those programs offer their students. This site includes information on related jobs, such as recording engineer, and provides definitions of the terms often used in the recording industry.

Music Gateway

www.musicgateway.com

The website includes helpful videos, lists of producer responsibilities and essential equipment, as well as explanations of the terminology used in the recording industry. There are also links to dozens of articles about creating a home studio, working with up-and-coming artists, and much more.

MUSIC TEACHER

People who love music and want to inspire others to feel the same way often become music teachers. Music teachers work at all levels of public and private education, from elementary schools up through colleges and music conservatories. Many music teachers also give private or group lessons outside of the school setting. Regardless of the work environment, music teachers often find the greatest rewards in passing along a love of music and watching their students build skills and memories to last a lifetime. "I hope the students take away a pile full of memories and good experiences," Nikki Bunnell, a vocal teacher at Mitchell High School in Mitchell, Nebraska, told the *Star-Herald* newspaper before directing her first musical, *Cinderella*, in 2021. "Just the opportunity to do these kinds of things, is always just a joy. I remember that being in high school. I have memories I hold on to from being in performances, so I hope they get to have a lot of good moments."[27]

What Does a Music Teacher Do?

At the elementary school level, a music teacher must be a jack of all trades, instructing students in singing and musical concepts such as pitch and rhythm. They also introduce students

A Few Facts

Typical Earnings
Average annual salary of $53,000

Educational Requirements
A bachelor's degree, usually in music or music education, and a teaching certificate

Personal Qualities
Wide-ranging musical knowledge, patience, organization, good communicator

Work Settings
Public or private K–12 schools, colleges, home studios

to various instruments and in some cases teach them to read music and dance. In middle and high school, music teachers tend to specialize in areas of singing (chorus), band (brass, woodwinds, and percussion), and orchestra (strings and percussion).

In addition to teaching classes all day, music teachers often have additional duties, such as leading the school's chorus, marching band, jazz band, and other performing groups. This can mean rehearsals after school or on weekends, traveling with students to music festivals and competitions, and conducting evening concerts at school or elsewhere in the community. "It's very much a full time job, 24-7," band director Chris Herrero of Edna Karr High School in New Orleans, Louisiana, told New Schools for New Orleans, a non-profit organization focused on school improvement and teacher retention in Louisiana's biggest city. "There's not a point in time that I'm not a band director. I might have a parent or student texting me at any time with a problem, and I do my best to help them out."[28]

At the college level, music instructors may teach even more specialized courses, focusing on a single instrument, such as the saxophone, or on a particular style of singing, such as opera. They are preparing the next generation of professional musicians, singers, and others who plan to make their career in music.

The Workday

Music teachers who work in schools usually work eight hours a day, five days a week, just like other teachers. Like other teachers, they create lesson plans and tests for each of their classes—often after school hours on their own time. That can be especially challenging for elementary school music teachers, who work with a wide range of ages and abilities. They may spend part of their day teaching kindergarteners a simple song or basic rhythms, third graders how to read music, and fifth graders basic songwriting.

The workday for music teachers differs depending on where they teach. Elementary school music teachers either have their own classroom and teach students from different classes and grades throughout the day or they move from one classroom to another for the day's music lesson. In some school districts, a music teacher might travel from one school to another. Middle and high school music teachers often have their own classroom and may teach general music classes that introduce students to different styles of music and basic music theory, or they specialize in teaching band, chorus, or strings.

As part of their regular schedule, high school band teachers, for example, may have classes of beginning band students, classes of mid-level students, and classes for more advanced music students. This might involve a jazz band, wind ensemble, or, as in the case of New York City band teacher Dana Monteiro, a fifty-student class devoted strictly to samba music. Monteiro decided to experiment with a samba class, partly because he thought his students would respond to the lively Brazilian music, but also because he had an oversized class filled with kids who wanted to be drummers. "Samba ensembles in Brazil can number over 200 drummers, so 50 students in a class works well," says Monteiro, who teaches at Frederick Douglass Academy in Harlem. "It has a low bar of entry, so every student can feel that they are contributing to the sound of the group. It also has a really high ceiling, so students with more experience and ability can achieve a very high level of playing."[29]

The workday for private music teachers might consist of a few hour-long lessons during the day, as well as evening sessions, particularly for adults learning an instrument. Private music instructors teach individuals and small groups. A day might consist of a lesson with a young beginning musician, followed by a more advanced high school student hoping to get a music scholarship to college, and then an older adult picking up an instrument decades after playing as a child.

Education and Training

Most music teachers have an undergraduate college degree in music or education, and many have a master's degree as well. Like

Inspiration from Students

"My students inspire me every day to try to be a better teacher. They motivate me to find innovative ways to keep them engaged in band. You don't want to keep doing the same old thing. You don't want to only do what you, as the band director, think is best for the band—they're in the band too, so their voice matters, their opinion matters."

—Band director at Lafayette Academy in New Orleans, Louisiana, Charles Jackson

Quoted in New Schools for New Orleans, "'Music Is in Our DNA': Band Directors on Values, Setlists, and the Arts in New Orleans," March 1, 2019. https://newschoolsforneworleans.org.

all school teachers, music instructors must obtain a teaching certificate. This is frequently earned while a future teacher is earning a bachelor's degree. Music teachers must also pass several exams in order to earn that certificate, including proficiency in their field.

Private music instructors may have a professional education background, but many are professional musicians who no longer perform regularly or who want to earn extra money on the side. Music educators teaching at the college level typically hold a PhD or other doctorate in musical arts.

Skills and Personality

Music teachers are usually proficient in at least one instrument, but many can play multiple instruments, so they can teach their students those instruments. Playing piano or keyboards is almost essential at the lower levels and for chorus teachers to accompany their students while they sing. A good music teacher is usually upbeat and able to play and sing all day to keep the students engaged and inspired.

Music teachers at the elementary and middle school levels must have the patience to teach students who love music, those who have no interest in the class, and plenty of kids in between.

A high school music teacher works with a student who is learning to play cello, while other students practice a piece they will eventually perform. Music teachers work in various settings, including schools, colleges, and in homes where they give private instruction.

Organizational and classroom management skills, especially amid the noise and activity of band practices and music classes, are also a must.

Working Conditions

School-based music teachers in middle and high schools usually have their own classrooms. Band and orchestra teachers often have large classrooms and must also be responsible for lockers that store musical instruments. At the elementary school level, music teachers may have their own classroom—usually filled with percussion instruments, a piano or keyboard, audio equipment, as well as chairs and music stands. But some elementary music teachers do not have their own room and travel to different classrooms each day, typically wheeling in a cart stocked with the items necessary for that day's lesson.

Well-funded schools can often supply most of what music teachers need to do their jobs, but educators frequently dip into their own funds to buy supplies or apply for grants to buy everything from bongos to ukuleles. Underfunded schools present even greater challenges for teachers trying to build strong music programs, since the arts typically are not spending priorities.

Those music educators who do not work in school settings are likely to work for themselves and teach students in their home, a local music store, a rented studio space, or a student's home. Private music teachers can set their own schedules, but they are dependent on having enough students to help keep their income up.

Employers and Earnings

Nearly 90 percent of K–12 music teachers work in public schools, while the remainder work in private schools or other school settings. Larger, wealthier public school districts are able to employ more music teachers than smaller school districts or those that are in less-affluent areas. Public school teachers are employed at specific schools (unless they rotate from school to school), but they are employees of the school district. Private school music teachers are employed directly by the school at which they teach or by a company that runs several private schools.

Teacher pay varies drastically from one region to another, but the Bureau of Labor Statistics reports that, on average, elementary school music teachers earn about $59,000 a year, while high school teachers make about $61,000. In states with a high cost of living, such as New York and California, high school music teachers often make more than $80,000 annually. Glassdoor.com and Salary.com estimate that private music instructors make an average of about $50,000 a year, again noting a wide disparity in income based in part on geography. At the college level, educators in music and the other arts make an average of $84,000, according the Bureau of Labor Statistics.

Future Outlook

The employment website CareerExplorer estimates that there are about 122,500 music teachers in the United States, with job

Making a Difference

"There is a certain indescribable wealth that comes as a bonus to every music educator's payment plan. It may be in the form of a parent who pulls you aside to tell you of the importance music plays in the role of his/her child's life. It may manifest itself as a holiday greeting card from a student from many years ago who poetically tells you of the values learned in your choir, and how those very values helped him complete medical school. It may be the smile of a fifth grader who quietly whispers in your ear, 'I like music better than anything else in school. Thank you.' And on, and on, and on."

—Music educator Tim Lautzenheiser

Quoted in National Association for Music Education, "Choosing Music Education as a Profession," 2021. https://nafme.org.

growth expected to add about 18,000 new positions in the next decade. But opportunities for music and other arts teachers are not equal across the country. Many school districts have cut back on arts programs for funding reasons. But as research continues to underscore the importance of music education in supporting other academic disciplines, such as mathematics, and in relieving student stress, some school districts are reinvesting in their music and art programs.

In its 2020 budget, for example, the School District of Philadelphia for the first time had per-student allotments specifically for art and music. Before then, schools could use money that might otherwise go to the arts for other purposes. One result of the city's bump in funding was the creation of a school-supported record label at George Washington Carver High School of Engineering and Science and the production of a record in 2021. "One of the missions of Carver is to make sure that every student has some way to live their passions," humanities teacher Christina Puntel told the *Philadelphia Inquirer* newspaper in June 2021. "We want kids to have something they love."[30]

Such encouraging developments are happening in many communities. Milwaukee voters approved a referendum in 2020 to help restore arts programs in schools that had been forced to cut them. In Vermont and other states, music teachers are helping their schools meet various state education requirements by incorporating science lessons and other subjects into their music classes. The bottom line is that music teachers are being recruited and retained because they are seen as essential components of a well-rounded education.

Find Out More

How to Become a Music Teacher, Teacher.org
www.teacher.org/career/music-teacher
This site explains the requirements to become a music teacher in every state and describes the job expectations at all levels of education. There are also links to various music educator organizations and information about teaching in other fields, too.

NAMM Foundation
https://www.nammfoundation.org
The National Association of Music Merchants (NAMM) operates a foundation that provides resources and information for music teachers and anyone else interested in furthering their music careers. Visitors to the site can read about studies supporting the importance of music education and learn more about the many types of music educators working today.

National Association for Music Education (NAFME)
https://nafme.org
Learn about programs such as the Tri-M Music Honor Society, state and national music competitions and scholarships, and opportunities to get involved in Music in Our Schools Month programs. The NAFME also conducts research about the importance of music education and provides news articles and tips for teachers in all disciplines of music.

MUSIC THERAPIST

Music therapy is a relatively new health field that uses music to help people with physical, psychological, cognitive, and social challenges. A music therapist, who is often a well-trained musician as well as a board-certified therapist, understands how music can bring about emotional responses that can relax, stimulate, or heal a person.

Music therapy can take on many forms, from playing music for clients to having the clients make music themselves. Music therapy is helpful for people with mood disorders, such as depression or anxiety, as well as those struggling with psychological trauma or even physical pain. Music therapy is also used to help older adults struggling with memory loss or other cognitive changes. Melanie Kwan, a music therapist working in Singapore, specializes in treating individuals struggling with chronic pain, many of them near the end of their lives. "Active music engagement allowed the patients to reconnect with the healthy parts of themselves, even in the face of a debilitating condition or disease-related suffering,"[31] Kwan says.

A Few Facts

Typical Earnings
Average annual salary of
$57,000

**Educational
Requirements**
A bachelor's or master's
degree in music therapy
or a related field

Personal Qualities
Musical skills, empathy,
creativity

Work Settings
Hospitals, schools,
nursing homes, private
mental health counseling
practices

What Does a Music Therapist Do?

Like any other type of therapist, a music therapist assesses the psychological and emotional needs of an individual by learning about the person's medical and mental health histories, current symptoms, and personality. Music therapy clients can include young children dealing with abandonment, abuse, or pain associated with cancer or other medical conditions. Likewise, a musical therapist can work with older kids, adults, and seniors coping with a wide range of challenges, such as memory loss, depression, or post-traumatic stress disorder (PTSD).

Once a music therapist understands the client's needs, he or she develops a treatment plan that might involve improvising music with clients or composing original songs. A music therapist might also play songs that trigger memories or motivate a person to talk about deep-seated feelings.

Music therapists may also teach clients to play an instrument. Drums in particular are effective at helping people express emotions without words. Drums and other music can be comforting as well. Music therapists often work with people suffering from chronic pain. Dr. Hilary Moss, with the music therapy program at the University of Limerick in Ireland, told the *Irish Times* that chronic pain sufferers need the comfort and joy that comes from making music. "Chronic pain is an invisible illness which can have catastrophic effects on work and social life, relationships and leisure interests," she says. "There is stigma and many people with chronic pain are not believed. The specific benefits we are seeing in music therapy is that it gives the opportunity to express yourself through music, allows you to tell your story and build hope and joy through enjoyable music making."[32]

The Workday

Music therapists see several clients a day, often in one-on-one sessions or in group sessions. The day may follow a typical nine-to-five schedule or include evenings to accommodate the needs of clients who work or go to school during the day. The workday includes time interacting with clients as well as time spent reviewing a client's case, consulting with that client's other therapists or doctors, and devising treatment plans.

The morning might start with a session with a group of veterans dealing with PTSD. Through a program called Guitars for Vets, music therapists are teaching vets how to play guitar and write songs to deal with their feelings. "When you put this guitar in the hands of somebody that is sinking deeply into depression, it opens up a window of serenity for them, enough that they can understand that they are capable of feeling good again,"[33] says Guitar for Vets cofounder Patrick Nettesheim.

Later in the day, a music therapist may sit down with a child who is anxious or unhappy at school and play the ukulele, teaching the young client a song while also discussing what is going on at school. After that, a music therapist might pack up some equipment and head over to a long-term-care facility for older adults, sitting them in a circle and playing some old standards from their youth. Hearing those songs again can get seniors to start sharing stories, often about events and people that might otherwise have been forgotten.

Each client has a unique set of needs, so a music therapist's day is often filled with a variety of tasks and goals. Julie Renato, an Arizona-based music therapist, says sessions and workdays are never the same because the needs of clients are unique and always changing. She says:

> Each session varies so widely; I work with kids from the first day of life to early adulthood with varied diagnoses and needs. Sometimes, if a patient's in pain, I play the guitar at bedside to help them calm down so they can sleep with a reduced need for medications. I can hum a lullaby to help an agitated infant receive treatment. Sometimes a session is an engaging one where we can use drums or shakers; sometimes with older kids, we work on songwriting to help them express their feelings. I can also support family bonding too; maybe just for a moment, a mom can hold her child while I sing, and feel a little more normal.[34]

In-Demand Profession

"Music therapists are increasing in demand. This is often the case if you work with certain populations such as seniors living in long-term care facilities. As we are seeing the number of older adults increasing overall in our population, so does the need for valuable services that improve their well-being, such as music therapy."

—Toronto music therapist Miya Adout

Quoted in "Music Therapist," Careers in Music, November 4, 2014. www.careersinmusic.com.

Education and Training

A music therapist typically earns a bachelor's degree and a master's degree in music therapy. However, music therapists sometimes start out with an undergraduate education in psychology or a related field, only to focus on music therapy for a master's degree. Holly Chartrand is a music therapist with the Environmental Music Program at Massachusetts General Hospital, but she started out as a vocalist, graduating from the Berklee College of Music. She switched career paths after realizing how much music could help others in need. "The favorite part of my job is seeing how big an impact music can have on someone who isn't feeling well,"[35] Chartrand said in an interview with Heartstrings, a foundation that provides musical instruments and instruction to veterans and others who can benefit from music therapy.

While earning a degree in music therapy, an individual must put in twelve hundred hours of clinical training in order to become a board-certified music therapist. Those hours are usually accrued over a period of nine to twelve months. Ongoing professional development is also required throughout a music therapist's career. Ongoing education typically includes attending conferences, seminars, and classes in which new treatment strategies and trends in health care are shared.

Skills and Personality

Music therapists, like other mental health professionals, must have empathy for their clients, as well as imagination and creativity to develop a treatment plan appropriate for the client's issues. Music therapists must also be talented musicians who can teach instruments or other musical concepts to people who may have no musical background.

Music therapists must also be excellent communicators with the ability to work collaboratively with other health care providers along with clients and their families. An interest in the latest developments in therapy will also be helpful.

Working Conditions

Music therapists may work in their own office, which can resemble a music classroom, complete with a piano, drums, and other instruments, as well as audio equipment to play and record music. Sometimes music therapists travel for their work, bringing their unique approach to wellness into a nursing home, assisted living facility, senior center, or even a correctional facility to help inmates deal with their psychological challenges. Sometimes music therapists see clients in their home or travel to other facilities to work with people who are not able to travel.

Music therapists can expect to work forty to fifty hours per week, working individually with clients or in group settings. In many cases family members are included in therapy sessions or are consulted before or after sessions. A music therapist may also work in a practice that offers various other types of therapy, so a music therapist may collaborate with a traditional psychologist in treating an individual.

Employers and Earnings

Music therapists are usually hired by an institution such as a hospital, nursing home, or rehabilitation center or by a mental health care practice. Eventually, some music therapists establish their

A music therapist plays guitar while her client accompanies her on bongos. Music therapy can bring about emotional responses that lead to relaxation, stimulation, and healing for clients with a variety of needs.

own private practice. The American Music Therapy Association reports that the average salary for a music therapist is nearly $57,000. A music therapist who moves up into a management position at a large practice or a health care institution could expect to earn a six-figure salary.

Future Outlook

Because music therapy is a burgeoning field, the outlook for opportunities is strong in the years ahead. It is now a widely accepted field of mental health, the American Psychological Association reports, and its use in helping people with chronic pain and other debilitating conditions means it is likely to be in demand everywhere. CareerExplorer projects job growth of nearly 7 percent through 2026. Becoming board certified in another aspect of

Assessing a Client's Abilities

"The therapist will measure the patient/client's musical abilities and preferences and incorporate those (if any) into therapy sessions. Sometimes music lessons help in achieving certain goals, and music lessons will be incorporated into therapy."

—California music therapist Andrea Scheve

Quoted in Abigail Bassett, "What Is Music Therapy?," Shondaland, August 10, 2020. www.shondaland.com.

mental health care, such as a clinical mental health counselor, will broaden a music therapist's job prospects. Music therapy techniques may be applicable in still other forms of counseling and mental health care.

Find Out More

American Music Therapy Association

www.musictherapy.org

Learn more about becoming a music therapist, the techniques that are used, the misconceptions about the practice, and the kinds of conditions that are helped by music therapy. The site also features articles about music therapy research and the future of this exciting and rewarding profession.

Music Therapy, GoodTherapy

www.goodtherapy.org/learn-about-therapy/types/music-therapy Read about the history of music therapy, the qualifications to become a music therapist, and what happens in a music therapy session. Visitors to the site can also learn about who can be helped by this treatment, as well as the limitations of music therapy.

10 Best Music Therapy Degree Programs in the USA, Careers in Music

www.careersinmusic.com/music-therapy-degree

In addition to a brief explanation of music therapy and its history, the information on this site offers advice on choosing a music therapy program in college. Visitors to the site can then find descriptions of some of the top music therapy programs in the country, as well as information about many other music-related career fields.

DJ

The term *DJ* originated in radio many years ago. The people who played records (vinyl discs) on the air were nicknamed disc jockeys, or DJs. And while radio stations still have DJs, more people today associate the word *DJ* with the person who provides the music for parties, festivals, clubs, weddings, and other events. DJs play familiar hits and songs by new artists, as well as compilations of samples from a wide variety of sources.

For creative people who like to experiment with songs and sounds, being a DJ is the perfect job, especially for those who have some showmanship, too. Crowds often look to the DJ to keep the party vibe going. Many DJs create and then play their own music, making them like the headlining musicians at a concert. Some DJs become well-known celebrities.

But most DJs do not become big stars. They may be fairly anonymous parts of a wedding or other event, but they get paid for entertaining the crowd with a collection of music they put together. "The best part is that I get to use my instincts and experience to be a part of a really memorable day—the party of someone's lifetime, perhaps,"[36] says New York City wedding DJ James Mulry.

What Does a DJ Do?

DJs provide the soundtrack for events as big as an outdoor music festival attracting thousands of people or as

A Few Facts

Typical Earnings
Average annual salary of $42,000

Educational Requirements
No formal education required

Personal Qualities
Creativity, extroversion, organization

Work Settings
Radio station, club, music festival, party

small as an intimate wedding or a company's holiday party. But the job involves much more than playing one song after another. A DJ mixes tracks and samples, sometimes using digital files made at a home studio but often created over the course of a *set*—the term DJs use to describe their session on the job. A DJ's show also includes scratching (moving a vinyl record back and forth on a turntable for a rhythmic effect), juggling (using two or more samples to create a unique mix), rapping, and other bits of showmanship.

International DJ Carola Pisaturo says that improvisation during a set keeps things interesting for her and the crowd. "I pack my vinyl so I know there are certain tracks I'll reach for at different stages of the night," she said in a 2021 interview. "But with my digital tracks I can be a bit more off the cuff. Providing the tracks work together, then [it's] all good; I prefer to slowly tell a story than dramatically switch from one sound to another."[37]

Part of a DJ's job is to pick up on the vibe and mood of an event and play the music that fits it—or play music aimed at changing the mood and making sure people are dancing or just having a good time. "My job is to take people on a musical journey and eliminate some of their stress," DJ Jeff Townes (aka DJ Jazzy Jeff) told the *Philadelphia Inquirer* in September 2020 before working his first big festival after the start of the COVID-19 pandemic. "You don't want to completely forget about what's going on. But this is going to be the first time being outside for me and for a lot of these people. I want everybody to throw their hands in the air and have a good time."[38]

The Workday

Most DJ sets take place at night, though there are plenty of daytime events that feature music curated by a professional DJ. If the set is at night, a DJ will spend part of the day catching up on any new music that might be right for the event. Then a DJ will assemble records and tracks that are most likely to be played that night. DJs need to have current hits ready to go, as well as crowd favorites and, depending on the venue, some original mixes.

At smaller events, a professional DJ may supply the sound system as well as the laptop, console, microphone, and other equipment. That means arriving at the event early in order to set everything up and run a sound check. At a club or other large venue, the sound system is already in place, so the DJ is only responsible for his or her own equipment and recordings. A set may last an hour or two or for much longer, well into the early morning hours.

Education and Training

A DJ's education is usually learning by doing. DJs may get some inexpensive equipment to start with and pick up tips and how-to knowledge wherever they can. "Lots of DJs, myself included, taught ourselves at home using tools on the internet, watching tutorials, and experimenting and learning from failure,"[39] DJ Lost Frequencies said in a 2021 interview.

There are also schools and online classes people can take to learn how to DJ. Interning or just helping out professional DJs is also one of the best ways to learn the job. Being up close while a DJ works and asking questions later is like a class in itself.

DJs typically start out working parties with their friends and small events, such as middle school or high school dances. As their skills improve, they can move up to bigger and better-paying gigs.

Skills and Personality

Technical skills with audio and recording equipment are a must, but a good DJ also has to be able to read people and pick up on the mood or feeling at an event. A DJ also has to be willing to go along with what an audience wants and not just play whatever he or she wants to play. "You might get requests," DJ Cut Chemist

Playing to the Crowd

"If you can be clever in your selections as well as your technique—and it doesn't mean you need to be super aggressive with scratching or juggling—but if you can blend stuff and, with each transition, get the people excited, if you can keep things on the up, mixing in measure, it really does help. But that's a pretty straightforward club-style technique: blending songs together and making the crowd cheer when the next song comes in."

—New York City DJ James Mulry

James Mulry, "How I Accidentally Became a Popular Wedding DJ—and Learned to Love It," *Vice*, October 5, 2016. www.vice.com.

told Careers in Music. "You don't want to be a DJ who doesn't play stuff that people want to hear and dance to and have a good time to, because that's why you're there. Being able to read a crowd and being able to make left turns upon request; that's a unique skill set."[40]

For radio DJs, as well as those working in-person events, being extroverted and enjoying the interaction with an audience is essential. For Eileen Barnett, a DJ at WTJU in Virginia, audience interaction was especially valuable during the COVID-19 pandemic. "It felt magical to be a radio DJ during the pandemic," she said on her station's website. "I feel honored to connect with others over the airwaves and provide such an important, creative community service during such a challenging time."[41]

Working Conditions

While listening to music and putting tracks together for a set usually takes place at a home studio, working at an event can place

Know the Music

"You need to have a feeling for music. The best is to have some music education, like playing a piano, to understand what you are mixing and what you are working with. A feeling for rhythm is very important for mixing as well, and you should be good in understanding new technologies for DJs. It's important to always be up to date and to understand new technical features fast."

—German-based DJ Plastik Funk

Quoted in Careers in Music, "How to Become a DJ," 2021. www.careersinmusic.com.

a DJ in a wide variety of locales. It could be in a huge club in a big city with hundreds of people on the dance floor or a small-town community center hosting a wedding or someone's birthday party. A DJ might work a set on a beachfront, a field hosting a music festival, a rooftop party, a homecoming dance in a high school cafeteria, or anywhere people are gathering for an event that demands a soundtrack.

Traditional DJs work in radio stations, though many of them also work live gigs in clubs and elsewhere. Some DJs work at the same club for months at a time, while others travel around to music festivals and clubs across the country and overseas. "Top DJs tour relentlessly, playing an all-nighter in Berlin one night and a beach party in Thailand two days later,"[42] music blogger Alison Stolpa wrote on the Careers in Music website.

Employers and Earnings

Many DJs are independent contractors; they work for themselves and are hired to work one event at a time. The average cost of a wedding DJ is about $1,200, according to the wedding website the Knot. DJs who primarily work small, local events often have a full-time job doing something else. DJing is a sideline gig that typically pays about $100 to $200 an hour.

Some DJs, however, are hired by a club as the "resident DJ," and they work several nights a week, like any other employee. Again, the pay range is considerable, but ZipRecruiter reports that the national average income for a club DJ is about $49,000 a year.

Traditional radio DJs may be full- or part-time employees of radio stations. The Bureau of Labor Statistics reports an average annual salary of about $42,000, though DJs who work other gigs along with their radio jobs can earn much more.

Future Outlook

Opportunities for club DJs and DJs who work various events will be stronger in cities where new venues are opening up and the population is increasing. DJs who broaden their skill set and are also rappers or producers can find more career options, though those jobs are also highly competitive.

Find Out More

Digital DJ Tips
www.digitaldjtips.com
This so-called Global DJ School has a little bit of everything, from troubleshooting sound equipment and the latest products on the market to mixing advice from the pros and preparing for your first gig. Visitors to the site can also learn a lot from the collection of tutorials, all written with beginners in mind.

How to Become a DJ: A Beginner's Guide, Passionate DJ
https://passionatedj.com/how-to-become-a-dj-ultimate-guide
This guide provides an introduction to the job of being a DJ and offers in-depth information on DJ software and hardware, how to record a mix, and how to get DJ gigs. The guide also helps visitors plan their next steps once they have learned the craft and are a working professional DJ.

How to Become a DJ, Careers in Music
www.careersinmusic.com/dj
Learn what it takes to become a DJ, as well as hear from professional DJs about everything from how much the job pays to the
skills needed to succeed. Visitors to the site can also find links to
articles about DJ equipment, the pitfalls of the music business,
and more.

SOURCE NOTES

Introduction: A Life in Song

1. Quoted in Alyssa Bailey, "Here's Lady Gaga's Moving Best Original Song Speech from the Oscars," *Elle*, February 25, 2019. www.elle.com.
2. Quoted in Lisa Petrillo, "'Chilling We Lost an Entire Year': Live Music Industry Hoping In-Person Performances Pick Back Up After Shutdown," WBFS-TV, March 15, 2021. https://miami.cbslocal.com.
3. Quoted in Naeisha Rose, "Hybrid Model Is the Future for an Arts Center," *New York City Queens Chronicle,* June 24, 2021. www.qchron.com.
4. Quoted in Andrew Chow, "'It Feels like I'm Chosen to Do This.' Inside the Record-Breaking Rise of Lil Nas X," *Time*, August 15, 2019. https://time.com.

Performer

5. Sharon Wehner, "Day-to-Day Life as a Professional Ballerina," *4dancers* (blog), April 9, 2017. www.4Dancers.org.
6. Douglas Yeo, "Pros and Cons to a Career in Orchestral Music," Douglas Yeo Trombone Web Site. www.yeodoug.com.
7. Quoted in Kristyn Brady, "What Dancers Can Do with a College Degree That They Can't Do Without One," Dance Spirit, August 15, 2018. www.dancespirit.com.
8. Quoted in Maggie Maloney, "Aretha Franklin's Most Iconic Quotes of All Time," *Town & Country*, August 26, 2018. www.townandcountrymag.com.
9. Quoted in *The Strad*, "Divide Your Practice into Hour-Long Chunks, Says Violinist Sarah Chang," March 25, 2015. www.thestrad.com.
10. Quoted in Holly Gleason, "The Pretty Reckless: Transforming Pain, Moving Forward," *American Songwriter*, May 2021. https://americansongwriter.com.

11. Quoted in Deepti Hajela, "Without Waiter Jobs, What Happens to Creative New York?," AP, July 15, 2020. https://apnews.com.

12. Quoted in Jon Haworth, "For Musicians and Artists, COVID-19 Pandemic Was a Turning Point," ABC News, February 14, 2021. https://abcnews.go.com.

Composer/Songwriter

13. Quoted in *Columbus (OH) Dispatch*, "From NINE to TITANIC and Beyond: A Talk with Broadway Composer Maury Yeston," August 8, 2010. www.dispatch.com.

14. Quoted in Heather Wood Rudolph, "Get That Life: How I Became a Hit Songwriter by Age 21," *Cosmopolitan*, November 2, 2015. www.cosmopolitan.com.

15. Quoted in Meryl Ayres, "From Sight to Sound: Composing Music for Film and TV," Wistia, July 20, 2015. https://wistia.com.

16. Quoted in Jeff Bond, "Top 25 Music Schools for Composing for Film and TV," *Hollywood Reporter*, November 16, 2018. www.hollywoodreporter.com.

17. Quoted in Freya Parr, "An Interview with Composer Philip Venables," *Classical Music*, August 17, 2018. www.classical-music.com.

18. Quoted in Scott Roxborough, "Composer Roundtable: Pros from 'Mank,' 'Soul,' 'Minari,' and More Talk Remote Recording Sessions and Finding Creativity in Isolation," *Hollywood Reporter*, January 26, 2021. www.hollywoodreporter.com.

Music Producer

19. Quoted in Karen Ponzio, "Sam Carlson Mixes It Up with Sans Serif Recording," *New Haven (CT) Independent*, November 27, 2018. www.newhavenindependent.org.

20. Quoted in Keith Nelson, "From Purge to Perfection: Illangelo on Producing the Weeknd's 'After Hours,'" *ProSound News*, June 7, 2021. www.prosoundnetwork.com.

21. Quoted in Nathaniel Puente, "RGV Sounds: Metal Producer Gets the Best Out of Bands in McAllen Studio," KVEO-TV, June 27, 2021. www.valleycentral.com.

22. Quoted in Careers in Music, "How to Become a Music Producer," January 20, 2021. www.careersinmusic.com.

23. JP Remillard, "A Day in the Life of a Music Producer," Pheek Mix & Mastering, January 6, 2017. https://audioservices.studio.

24. Quoted in Careers in Music, "How to Become a Music Producer."

25. Quoted in Dharmic X, "Dr. Dre Talks Working with Eminem, Race, and Staying Up 79 Hours Nonstop to Make Music," Complex Music, December 11, 2013. www.complex.com.

26. Quoted in Careers in Music, "How to Become a Music Producer."

Music Teacher

27. Quoted in Lauren Brant, "Mitchell Vocal Music Teacher Brings Experience to 'Cinderella,'" *Scottsbluff (NE) Star-Herald*, April 8, 2021. https://starherald.com.

28. Quoted in New Schools for New Orleans, "'Music Is in Our DNA': Band Directors on Values, Setlists, and the Arts in New Orleans," March 1, 2019. https://newschoolsforneworleans.org.

29. Quoted in Pooja Salhotra, "With Samba, This Harlem Music Teacher Turned a 50-Student Class into an Asset," Chalkbeat, July 9, 2021. https://ny.chalkbeat.org.

30. Quoted in Kristen A. Graham, "These Philly Teens Wanted In on the Music Business. Now, They Have Their Own Record Label," *Philadelphia Inquirer*, June 28, 2021. www.inquirer.com.

Music Therapist

31. Quoted in Amy Novotney, "Music as Medicine," American Psychological Association, 2013. www.apa.org.

32. Quoted in Sylvia Thompson, "'The Drums Sounded like Ocean Waves': How Music Therapy Can Help Chronic Pain Sufferers," *Irish Times* (Dublin, Ireland), October 11, 2020. www.irishtimes.com.

33. Quoted in Joel Waldinger, "Guitars for Vets: The Healing Power of Music in the Hands of Heroes," *Wisconsin Life*, October 27, 2016. https://wisconsinlife.org.
34. Quoted in Phoenix Children's Hospital Foundation, "Music Therapy: An Essential Instrument in the Healing Process," 2021. https://phoenixchildrensfoundation.org.
35. Quoted in Heartstrings, "How Music Can Help You Heal," February 26, 2018. https://heartstringsfoundation.org.

DJ

36. James Mulry, "How I Accidentally Became a Popular Wedding DJ—and Learned to Love It," *Vice*, October 5, 2016. www.vice.com.
37. Quoted in Fifteen Questions, "Fifteen Questions Interview with Carola Pisaturo," 2021. https://15questions.net.
38. Quoted in Dan DeLuca, "For DJ Jazzy Jeff and Son Cory, Labor Day Jam Will Be a Family Affair," *Philadelphia Inquirer*, September 4, 2020. www.inquirer.com.
39. Quoted in Careers in Music, "How to Become a DJ," 2021. www.careersinmusic.com.
40. Quoted in Careers in Music, "How to Become a DJ."
41. Quoted in WTJU 91.1 FM, "Host Profile: Eileen Barnett," February 7, 2021. www.wtju.net.
42. Quoted in Careers in Music, "How to Become a DJ."

INTERVIEW WITH A MUSIC TEACHER

Victor Mongillo has been a high school band director in Sarasota, Florida, for more than twenty years. He answered questions about his career by email.

Q: Why did you become a music teacher?
A: I was extremely fortunate to have been taught by outstanding music educators, from 5th grade through 12th. Their passion and skill was second to none, and even at a young age I remember thinking, what a wonderful life they have!

Q: Can you describe your typical workday?
A: Most days I would arrive 1–2 hours before my first class and start with reviewing scores and sections of pieces we are rehearsing. The rehearsal plan for the day could be altered depending on how the pieces were proceeding. Many days could also include listening to additional works of music, meeting with students for solo and ensemble help, paperwork for band events, trip planning, copying parts, helping beginners, scheduling/meeting with coaches, practicing trumpet, etc.

Q: What do you like most about your job?
A: Answering this question should be easy, but there is so much I love and enjoy about my job. For me, it wasn't only that I loved playing trumpet and wanted to be the best musician I could be, but it's a very special feeling to be part of a group of young people that are striving for a collective goal; to communicate through sound while striving for something special, even beautiful. The connections young people make through performing ensembles often last a lifetime and my best friends, still to this day, are musicians I met

in middle and high school band. Although only a small portion of students will go on to study music and even create wonderful careers in the performing arts, the vast majority of students will go on to other professions but often relate to me how their experiences in band helped shape who they are and how they connect with others with common goals, desires and even dreams once imagined and brought to fruition.

Q: What do you like least about your job?

A: Having to prove the value of performing arts as an equal component in a child's education year after year. The performing arts doesn't fit in the box of "testable" results, and success is often a feeling. The feeling that spontaneous applause brings after a piece is well played. The feeling of your ensemble receiving first place in a competition. The feeling of traveling together to wonderful places in which thousands of like-minded young musicians gather to make beautiful music. These are immeasurable and will not show up on the radar of those deciding what should be cut or underfunded.

Q: What personal qualities do you find most valuable for this type of work?

A: Patience, perseverance, organizational skills and a deep desire to wish success for all students. Although traits of the "good" teacher do overlap in many aspects of teaching, the performing arts teacher often deals with educational extremes. Academically speaking, a student at an Algebra 1 level would never be placed in calculus or an Introduction to Spanish student wouldn't be scheduled in a Conversational Spanish class. Yet, this happens often in the performing arts setting. We must adapt and not only include the student but find a path in which they can succeed and even thrive. Classes are often 50-plus students, which not only creates a logistical challenge but often an "unbalanced" ensemble. Performing arts teachers are always re-writing pieces and re-thinking ways to keep the composer's intentions intact. We also become salesmen—constantly finding ways to fund the program and the challenges that come with quality instruments and music costing thousands of dollars. The success of a group often comes down to how rehearsals are scheduled, which makes working together with administration every year crucial. Most of these skills and necessary traits are rarely approached in the education received in college. It all comes back to finding a way to do what we need to do to give our students a special place in their day. A place where they can breathe a little and enjoy making beautiful sounds with their classmates and belonging to something they will hopefully take with them for the rest of their lives.

Q: What advice do you have for students who might be interested in this career?
A: Much of what you will learn at the university level preparing you for the profession are guidelines, but flexibility is crucial. Never lose sight of why you wanted to do this—your love of music. You will change children's lives and hopefully give them a gift they will have forever.

OTHER JOBS IF YOU LIKE MUSIC

Artist agent
Artist manager
Artists and repertoire (A&R)
  representative
Audio engineer
Booking agent
Choreographer
Concert hall manager
Concert promoter
Instrument technician
Musical instrument builder/
  designer
Music arranger

Music director/conductor
Music festival director
Music journalist
Music photographer
Music publicist
Music publisher
Music store owner/staff
Music supervisor for film and TV
Radio music director
Recording studio manager
Sound technician
Talent agent
Vocal coach

Editor's note: The online *Occupational Outlook Handbook* of the US Department of Labor's Bureau of Labor Statistics is an excellent source of information on jobs in hundreds of career fields, including many of those listed here. The *Occupational Outlook Handbook* may be accessed online at www.bls.gov/ooh.

Cover: Shootdiem/Shutterstock.com

11: By Eric Fahrner/Shutterstock.com
32: Monkey Business Images/Shutterstock.com
41: Miriam Doerr Martin Frommherz/Shutterstock.com

James Roland started out as a newspaper reporter more than twenty-five years ago, and then moved on to become an editor, magazine writer, and author.